# Most of What We Take Is Given

a poetic sequence

by

Stephen E. Smith

Singular Speech Press

Canton, Connecticut

## Acknowledgments

Some of these poems have been previously published in the following magazines: *Cairn, The Cape Rock, Green River Review, Southern Poetry Review, Apalachee Quarterly, Muse, Poets On, The Arts Journal, Buffalo Spree, Loblolly, Passion for Industry, Interim, The Montana Review, Quarterly West* and *St. Andrews Review.*

"Michael," "Most of What We Take Is Given," and "Coming Back to the Old Emptiness" appeared in the *Anthology of Magazine Verse and Yearbook of American Poetry,* 1985, 1986, 1989.

"Cricket Poem" and "Michael" appeared in *Light Year* 1985, 1987, Bits Press, Case Western Reserve University.

"Saturday, June 19, 1954" and "Saturday, June 19, 1965" were published as broadsheets by North Carolina Wesleyan College.

"Photograph: Breezewood, 1951," "A Brief History of the Sixties," "Cricket Poem," and "Fluid Drive" appeared in *The Bushnell Hamp Poems*, Green River Press, 1980, and are included as part of this poetic sequence.

Some of these poems and accompanying songs are available on audio tape from Offbeat Studio, 965 Old US 1 South, Southern Pines, North Carolina 28387.

All characters in these poems are imaginary.


Copyright © 1991 by Stephen E. Smith
ISBN 1-880286-05-X

*to Leonard Price McKnett, Sr. and Margaret Smith McKnett*

# Contents

The 1950s 1
Photograph: Breezewood, 1951 3
Advice 4
Saturday, June 19, 1954 6
The Day Uncle Tully Told Me
About Flying Saucers 8
Bark 10
A Three-D Afternoon in Easton, Maryland,
Circa Sept. 1956 12
Whatever There Was To Say 13
Delmarva 15
My Grandfather Ties My Tie 17
Scar 18
Cleaning Pools 19
Crying in Miss Judy's Class 21
Christmas Poem 22
Nothing 24
Michael 25
The Fence 27
A Brief History of the Sixties 30
The Poet in My Tenth Grade English Text 32
Cricket Poem 33
Fluid Drive 35
Saturday, June 19, 1965 36
For a Fifty-Three Dodge 38
Short Note on a Cat Sleeping 39
Senior Talent Night 40
Working for Dorsey 42

I Visit Nancy Simmons at a Catholic Girls'
College, Saturday, April 26, 1969   44
The Great Depression   46
How the World's Been Treating Them: January, 1970   48
No Photograph   50
Wine and Cliches   52
Coming Back To the Old Emptiness   54
Most of What We Take Is Given   56

# The 1950s

To know how it was in the fifties
go to the nearest pay phone,
deposit a dime
and call home when you know
no one is there.

While the phone is ringing,
shut your eyes and imagine
at the other end of the line
daffodils and sunlight
(it is always a spring morning
in the fifties).

Recall whatever pleases you:
pineapple upside down cake,
Rosemary Clooney, Glass Wax,
a blue checkered tablecloth,
Almond Roca, HaloLights,
Gunther Beer, I Like Ike
buttons, Pablum, Ann Blyth,
tangerines —

but you must allow the phone
to ring for ten years.
When no one answers,
you'll know you've dialed
the right number.

## Photograph: Breezewood, 1951

Spring-blasted Ohio farms blurred turquoise
against the isinglass. Just out of Pittsburgh
Rt. 30 swayed into the Alleghenies where gorges
oozed acid from their running sores.

The child I was traced the journey with a
nickel's edge, counted towns that resolved
from map specks into winks in the rear-view
mirror. We cleared Greensburg and Boswell
before Bedford brought down the night.
The Crosley's highbeams touched the edge
of earth, airport beacons raked the astonished
horizon. Then the lights of Breezewood bluely
domed the sky, lifted the curtain, took us in.

Beneath the green and red crackle of a neon sign
we ate chicken in a basket, drank milkshakes.
Before that final departure, my mother produced
a Kodak and shanghaied an obliging vagrant
who flashed a photograph

of a time we would not come back from. Thirty
years are trembling in these paralytic smiles,
the gravel sharp eyes, the casual faces we wore,
these three shadows that sudden light lays bare
to bone.

## Advice

A full moon rose
through the chain-link fence
as my father lifted me over.
The Country Club pool
had been closed since dark,
but there we stood
staring into the pure
star-glazed water of the rich.
"We're as good as they are,"
my father whispered.

He plunged in naked.
I climbed the steel ladder
to the top of the high dive,
crawled to the board's
sandpaper edge and looked down.
What I saw was the bright
moon-struck face of a poor man
who'd had it up to here.
"Jump!" he yelled.

I told the truth: "I'm scared!"
"Listen," he called back,
"you'll never get anywhere
in this life unless you take
a chance once in a while!"
It was the only advice
the old man had ever given me:
I flung myself feet first
into the dark.

Believers, it was like no leap
a poet ever leapt.
I did not hang suspended—
even for a moment—
in the blue drift of air.
I did not see before me
the confused unfolding
of my life, nor could I hear
the voice of Danny Chapman
daring me, ten years later,
to take the Newcomb Turnoff
at ninety. I did not feel
the splintered bones,
the broken promises, the blackened
eyes, the lost love. And I sure
as hell never saw the fist
that would one night extract
three of my teeth in the alley
behind Sam Lorey's Tavern.

No, I dropped straight down
and sank into black water, belched
air at dead bottom, then clawed my
way back to the night's thin surface.
I looked up into the Milky Way
and saw the bare stars
fewer than my mistakes.
"Help me! Help me!" I screamed.
And from the dark I heard
my father's voice.
"Boy," he said, "you jumped in,
you get yourself out."

# Saturday, June 19, 1954

I ate Wheaties for breakfast and about nine BT came over and we got my father's car wax and polished our bikes. Then we rode down to Danny Chapman's house and played Korea for about two hours. BT and Danny got in an argument about whether dead commies pull triggers and Danny got BT down on the ground and put his knees on BT's shoulders and wouldn't let him up till Danny's mother came out and said she couldn't stand it anymore, to let BT up or she'd call our mothers and we wouldn't be able to play together again, ever.

My mother fixed minute steak sandwiches for lunch and then I had to take a polio nap. It was hot in the bedroom and my sister kept laughing and Mother came in and said that we'd get polio and spend the rest of our lives in wheel chairs if we didn't shut our eyes and get our proper rest and is that what we wanted, to spend our lives as cripples, but it didn't make any difference, my sister started snickering as soon as Mother had closed the door.

About three Mother said that if we wanted to get polio it was all right with her but not to blame her because she tried, so we went outside and my sister stepped on a bee and got stung and spent the rest of the day crippled. BT thought it was funny that someone else got hurt and then we went down to the Texaco Station and bought ice cream sandwiches and watched Charlie Truette change tires. Charlie didn't like BT, so he bent back BT's fingers till he screamed uncle six times and cried. Then we went home for supper.

We had liver, which I spit out when no one was looking and stuffed into the pocket of my shorts. I ate the butter beans and potatoes and drank the Kool-Aid. The Jello hadn't set, so we didn't have any dessert. Mother said we could play till dark and my sister wanted to collect lightning bugs so she could make a lamp for her room. But for some reason there weren't any lightning bugs that night and BT said it was a dumb idea anyway. At dusk Mother called us in and I took a bath and checked my head for ticks. Mother found the liver in my pocket and said that babies were starving to death in Europe and flushed the liver down the toilet. I asked her to read me a story but she said I hadn't eaten my supper so she wouldn't and she turned off my bedroom light. I didn't care; it had been a pretty good day.

# The Day Uncle Tully Told Me About Flying Saucers

"They come in over Knot's barn
looking like the hubcaps
off your daddy's Henry J,"
Uncle Tully whispered,
"and there's these little
green men inside who'll
snatch you up and take you
God knows where
if you stay out after dark."

I was seven years old the day
Uncle Tully told me
about flying saucers
and that night I prayed that I'd
not be taken.
"Jesus," I whispered, "save me
from the little green men."
And just to make sure
I stayed away from Knot's barn
after dark.

This morning,
as I ascend thirty-two floors
in as many seconds,
a blue-serge lady in the
elevator reads aloud from
a tabloid a story about
two Mississippi men abducted
by creatures from outer space.
"God save us from that,"
she says.

Then I'm alone
in the corridor —
the piped-in music,
the fluorescent lights,
my wing-tipped oxfords
on the blue carpet —
I'm remembering
Uncle Tully,
all my prayers,
and wondering what in God's
name ever became of me.

# Bark

I brushed aside the wild clover
and wormed into a culvert on a July
afternoon because my brown and white
springer spaniel had disappeared
into the other end.

I called, "Here boy!"
and heard his bark rattled down
the corrugated pipe, saw in flickering
light that dog waddle toward me
through tangles of sage
and roadwire, tongue dangling,
light ovaled in his brown eyes.

That December my spaniel was lost.
Hunkered beneath the porch light,
his clouded breath drifting,
my father told me, "That dog is gone
for good; you aren't ever going
to see him again."

But I did: in dead February
I skated onto Paper-Mill Pond
and stopped to stare deep into
ice dark as any hurt.
Saw there an ear, one brown eye
staring skyward, a paw pressed cold
against my hand.

The weather warmed, the bruise
darkened and belly down I crawled
onto the rotten ice
the very afternoon my springer
rose finally into light —
eyes gone milky, fur matted,
tongue twisted purple.
"Here boy," I whispered,
just as his death burst
into the April air.

# A Three-D Afternoon in Easton, Maryland, Circa Sept. 1956

Danny Chapman's big brother George
tears my matinee ticket, hands me
the stub and the folded three-D glasses.
I descend the velvet roped aisle
into the Avalon Theatre, grey rainlight
from beyond the padded double doors
fading like last week's coming
attractions.

Stampeding buffalo tumble into the
orchestra pit. Tommy Hash, a year
older than I and in Miss Judy's
fourth grade class, lifts his glasses
up and down. "Jeez, neat!" he
whispers. We applaud for the credits.
George holds the EXIT door open and
I'm in the street,

the three-D glasses still on my face.
The sky is a red quilt of clouds and
Garrison's Hobby Shop is blurring out
of business just beyond my father's
red two-tone Chevy idling at the curb.

I have caught my ole man red-faced,
his hand on the gearshift knob.
"How's the world look through those
glasses?" he asks, dropping it into
first. "Jeez, neat!" I answer, as
we run the red light at the corner
of Dover and Harrison.

## Whatever There Was To Say

*A sky the pallor of hands folded in a casket.*

You are driving south on Church Street this November
afternoon, and as you approach a railway crossing,
you notice a family, or what you believe
to be a family, walking the road — a man, a woman,
a boy, and a small girl, who is maybe eight.
The girl wears a blue print dress and is barefoot
in this late chill. And because the sky is the gray
of your grandmother's hands, you recall how that
old woman embraced you years ago as you sat in the
Avalon Theatre watching the movie news, the face
of a shivering child, a girl about the age of this
small girl, waiting beside a death camp railway.
Your grandmother put her arms around you there in
the darkness and you were embarrassed, felt awkward:
an old woman clinging to you, a child of eight,
in a crowded theatre. But your grandmother is a long
time dead and you have come to understand that shoeless
children are, these days, simply shoeless children:
you've seen so many and so much worse.

Yet there is something about this family,
this child, her straight yellow hair cut
at such a ragged angle, the thin face, eyes set
deep in shadow. And her brother in a green cap,
her father, tight-waisted in blue trousers,
the mother in a heavy, white-flecked overcoat.
They carry plastic bags filled with aluminum cans
gathered from the roadsides and ditches. And haven't
you seen these very faces in photographs of Jews,
Gypsies, Poles, eyes blank with resignation, fatigue,

awaiting the gas chamber, clutching their belongings —
as if those few scraps of cloth could be of some value
where they were going?  You wonder about this family,
wonder if the future of this small girl is as clear
as the past in photographs.  Wonder how these church
steeples dare to rise straight into the smoky skies
of this most terrible of centuries.  How neatly they
weave themselves among the bare branches of oak and
sycamore!  And haven't you finally come to understand
that whatever there was to say cannot be said?
Which is probably what your grandmother was telling
you in the darkness of that long ago matinee
when she held you hard against her as you watched
that child shivering beside the death camp railway.
Remember how you tried to pull away and how she held
on tight, as if that simple, desperate gesture
might make a difference in such a world?

## Delmarva

Child of wind and dark water,
I'd wander out under the clear dome
of stars and ask myself *Where am I?*
*How is it I came to be here?*
And when the inevitable chill
of isolation gripped me,
I'd recall the night my grandfather
walked in waist-deep snow
from Trappe Station to Oxford
and how a country he knew in his very bones vanished —
roads, trees, houses, fields —
all of it buried beneath a drifting landscape.
I'd look up into that random scattering of light
and tell myself: *I am here.*

Which is what my grandfather screamed
into a bitter wind knifing off the Chesapeake,
the path he'd struggled gradually effacing itself
and the night gone dead to language.
He'd tell me sometimes how,
without even the stars to guide him,
he knew precisely where he was,
knew every field and tree,
knew the houses and the roads
that lay beneath the drifts.
He could never explain how or why
he was blessed with such knowledge:
*Wasn't anything I thought,* he'd say,
*it was something I just felt.*

*Something I just felt,* I'd say the words
over and over as skeins of discordant geese
drifted down upon the Tred Avon
and a small wind rattled the marsh grass.
I'd scuff the peninsula
still firm beneath my feet
and stare into the winter sky,
the cold stars etched above me,
impassive but persistent.

## My Grandfather Ties My Tie

This morning it has to do
with my grandfather's breath
warm on my neck,
his pale eyes in the mirror
as he ties my tie.

It has to do
with his fingers fluttering
lightly against my chest,
the quick flick of silk
up and over and around,
his chin pressing too
firmly on my shoulder.

It has to do with me alone
in the mirror this morning
and his breath still warm,
his eyes my eyes,
his fingers fluttering
against my chest
as he chokes the knot
up tight and whispers,
"You look mighty sharp."

## Scar

From the high branches of mimosa
I look down and see BT Barnhart,
his arm already cocked,
the gray pointed roadrock
held lightly in his hand.
His arm snaps
and the rock floats up,
tumbling into memory.

There is time enough to move,
time to slide easily aside,
to hear the rock rattle among
the branches, the pink blossoms
exploding in the August dusk.

But I do not move
and these thirty years later
cannot explain why.
Each morning's mirror
asks that question
of the small triangular scar
below my left eye
which like regret
grows darker with age.

# Cleaning Pools

*to my father*

That summer you hired out to clean swimming pools
up and down the Delmarva in your Willys truck,
the back end clanking with pumps and pipes,
cans of HTH, diatomaceous earth and alum,
and hauled me along to skim from the chlorined
waters hopeless, deluded toads and the clotted
bodies of insects.

I was ten that summer but can remember
how the surface of each pool was a surprise,
the water still clear or gone cloudy,
the blue bottoms flecked with algae
and the shimmering coins I retrieved for baloney
sandwiches and sodas at the Royal Oak Grocery.
You'd place a hand on my shoulder and say,
"Dive deep and get us that lunch money."

It's been thirty years, but I often think of
those days, the hundred pound drums we toted,
the pump vomiting brown water, the ninety-nine
degree afternoons spent rolling rubber paint
on the walls of concrete craters — and especially
the empty tonic glasses, their sprigs of sere mint,
the careless underwear, the brown grass beneath
a mildewed towel some rich kid discarded.

Do you recall that August afternoon at the Talbot
County Country Club, the thirty-six filter bags
we pulled and laundered, the steel rings so tight
our fingers bled? It was a five-hour job
and when the bags and screens were back in place,
you dropped a pipe wrench clanging to the
bottom.

It was five more hours in the high beams
and neither of us spoke till the filter
lid was clamped and screwed down tight.
Then we leaned against the truck and shared
a warm soda. Sheet lightning streaked
over the Chesapeake, and I began to notice
how after each flash, I went momentarily blind.
"It's strange," you said, finally, and without
my having spoken a word, "how quickly the pupil
closes to the light and how complete the
darkness is. It must be like dying."

Tonight I watch a storm gather over Carolina,
the lightning so intense the billowing undersides
of clouds are illumined from horizon to horizon,
each flash stealing me into shadow. Perhaps,
as you said, it is like death, this sudden light
and inevitable darkness. Or perhaps it is the
purest grace. It says what fathers and sons
mostly cannot say: it is the quick chill of a hand
on my shoulder, it is like plunging deep
into the pure, blue waters of the rich.

## Crying in Miss Judy's Class

"Russian children never cry!"
Miss Judy screamed
after I broke down
in the fourth grade
having spelled separate
with three e's
on the same day sputnik
went into orbit
my father a school teacher
and me the dumbest kid
in the class
Jesus!

Later
when the poems
no one ever noticed
began to appear
I would imagine Miss Judy
leading the class in single file
all of them grown now into
Tupperware ladies and mobile
home salesmen
to the local bookstore.

"Look!" she screams
pointing at my poems waiting
in the window.
"There he is
the boy who pretended
to be so sensitive
grown up into a Communist!"

## Christmas Poem

I cannot write a Christmas
poem for you,
not with all those slick verses
oozing through the mail,
the schmaltzy music whining
on the radio.

But what I can do
is tell you of a December
afternoon in 1957
when I sat in Miss Judy's
fourth grade class
listening to the radiators clank
and staring at my scarred desktop
and how Danny Chapman,
hunched in the seat beside me,
looked up suddenly and whispered,
"It's snowing!"

I looked up too,
along with the rest of the class,
out the tall warped windows,
across the empty playground
to Idlewild Avenue,
and saw that it was true:
the first graywhite dust just drifting
the blue cedars.

If you are an old believer,
even on this bluest of December days,
I would give you that pale afternoon,
the chalkdust scuffle of shoes
on the worn floor,
those children's faces
eager as light.

# Nothing

We are driving east on Glebe Road
when a rabbit is caught
in the sudden snare of headlights.
My father eases off the gas,
downshifts, and the rabbit escapes
into marsh grass.
I'm twelve years old
and can think of nothing
but Nancy Simmons naked,
how at Paper-Mill Pond
I'd heard her laughter
and seen her pale body hidden
among the bleached reeds.
My father asks what I am thinking
and I cannot tell him
of breasts ripening
somewhere in this soft darkness.

Twenty-five years
and I'm driving with my son
on a summer night.
In the radio's blue glow
I see on his face
that look I could not see on my own:
the eyes of a startled animal,
life bearing down
with the instancy of light.
"What are you thinking?" I ask,
and he answers as we all must,
"Nothing."

# Michael

Received your letter today
and though we must live with what we've become
I was reminded of that July afternoon
Mother dropped us at the Cambridge Skating Rink
and said to me, "Stay with your brother;
he's only six."

I did, too,
though Cathy Baker, her new breasts blooming
beneath a blue cashmere sweater,
skimmed a seductive orbit
just beyond my longing.
Stayed with you during the ALL SKATE
and the COUPLES ONLY and the twelve trips
to the snack bar for lemonade
and then to the men's room where we stood
balancing before the porcelain,
suffocating slowly in the sour drift
of urinal cakes.

I was there, Michael, maybe imagining
Cathy Baker hunkered on wheels, one foot extended,
or pirouetting center floor, floating
languidly backward, her girl's body half
out of control, when what must happen to everyone
who ceases motion happened to you: the world
rolled out from under. And to save your life
you put both hands in the urinal.

I had not yet learned the body is a vessel
we are passing through, and as you looked up at me,
your eyes groping for salvation, your pink
fingers frozen among the soggy cigarettes
and dead gum, I thought you were ruined forever.

Perhaps, as you said in your letter, this life
of averages spares no one, but I remember how
even at six you were you, and how solemn you seemed
when you asked me, "Want some spearmint?
How about a Lucky Strike?"

# The Fence

Having sneaked our first cigarettes —
menthol filter-tipped Kools
we puffed like pros beneath
a broken moon — Danny and
I found ourselves astride
a picket fence just one block
from our empty beds when a bony
blue tick named Duke barked.
He was answered by a sooner
in the next county who awakened
a bitch up on Harrison Street, etc.,
until the night was a chorus
of mongrels gospeling.
Doors and windows jammed open,
lights flooded the darkness,
and we sat trembling astride that fence
not knowing which way to fall.

I tumbled to one side,
Danny to the other,
and we lay still as dead men
while flashlights ogled the damp grass,
danced among the limbs of cedars,
clattered along the picket fence
just inches above our faces
buried in the fetid glistening
of spring onions.
We did not draw breath
until one by one the lights had died,
and the barking trailed into echo.

Later we bragged,
slapped backs and laughed
as we told friends of our escape,
how we'd outwitted man and beast
by just keeping our cool and knowing
that eventually it would all go away,
that no one would remember
those doors thrown open into darkness
or the children we once had been.

## A Brief History of the Sixties

### I

When I was sixteen, my girlfriend
moved with her parents to California.
We said goodbye, embracing in front
of her locker at the high school.
This was in '64, near the end of
October.

It rained every day in November.
I went for long walks and wrote her
this line: "Rain makes the distance
seem less immense." Jesus, something
so sad had a beauty all its own.
Then I received a letter.

Stephen, it read, I love California.
I've got this neat tan. My hair
is getting really long. Just seems
like I stuffed my past in that locker
and slammed the door. This will be
my last letter. Out here the sun
shines forever.

### II

Linwood Thompson received his draft notice
in February of '67. "I feel like I'm
on board the Hindenburg about to dock
at Lakehurst," he said.

Yanked from his seat in American History,
he was the first to go. The names of
the missing began to echo down the open
ranks of desks. About a month before
he was killed, Linwood wrote from Khe Sanh:

On patrol I see myself down the sights
of someone else's rifle. Each day
comes now like a breath not taken.

# The Poet in My Tenth Grade English Text

There were big color photographs of him
hugging children and looking quizzical
as he bent over his notebook, pencil poised

and some candid shots of him buying
fruit at the local market and running his finger
along the spines of rare books in an antique
shop.

He never worked or worried about money.
He was always smelling flowers and staring
pensively out to sea just as the sun set.
Then they printed a poem he had written,
not one word of which I can now recall.

But I do remember closing my text
and thinking: What a racket!

## Cricket Poem

Swerving right at the corner of
Bay Ridge and Melrose,
I grabbed a crippled five-legger
as he stumbled the Dodge floorboard.
The other ninety-nine crickets,
purchased for fish bait at Barlow's,
spilled from their coffin
into Saturday sunlight
and scurried off beneath
dash padding and seat backs.
I sat with the car door open,
that five-legged jiminy tapping
encyclopedia into my palm,
and wondered what ninety-nine
crickets could do to a Dodge.

Nancy Simmons and I went
down that night with the *Thresher*
deep into the sea-green back seat
of that fifty-three Dodge.
Off Chinquapin Round Road
the news died whining on the car radio
and I pleaded like a doomed sailor.
She was about to moan yes
when a cricket whispered in her ear
and another called from
the glove compartment.

Suddenly her sisters were singing
in sun visors,
her mother cajoling from beneath
the clutch plate,
her father screaming in the dome light,
cousins chittering in the heater vents,
neighbors gossiping behind
the dashboard,
the cricket tabernacle choir singing
in ninety-nine part harmony
Nancy Nancy Nancy Nancy
save yourself forever.

# Fluid Drive

Beneath my eyelids the instinct arched.
Nancy, we made air dances of the rung-dry
night, a frenzied jungle-limbed fandango
in the front seat of my fluid drive Dodge.

Undreaming beneath me you were the old
felt self made suddenly sure. You hummed
"A Rose and a Baby Ruth" and I swooned
in the radio's blue light, my foot braced
against the deluxe heater.

In that perilous moment I rode that kite-
strung cradle, blood and bone wedged into
the wind, while Jurassic semi's groaned
south on John Hanson Highway.

You made me feel so damn good I cranked
up that flat-head six and let it blast
to screaming blue blazes, emptied out
my pure self into one brightly astonished
night

shuddering on firewheels, fluid drive and
a dollar gas.

# Saturday, June 19, 1965

I ate Wheaties for breakfast and about nine Danny Chapman came over and we got my father's car wax and polished my '53 Dodge. We had dates for the drive-in and thought our chances were better if the car looked real sharp, so we compounded the finish and buffed on double turtle wax. I got my mother's Electrolux and vacuumed the carpet and scrubbed the mats. Danny shined the chrome and I cleaned the windows with Glass Wax. Then we got some tire paint and blacked the sidewalls.

We went to McDonalds for lunch and got burgers, fries and shakes and listened to WCAO on the radio and watched girls drive through. I told Danny that if he didn't want to be a car suck he ought to give me a buck fifty for gas and oil but Danny said he'd be a little short, so we went to his house and poured in the gasoline his father kept for the lawn mower. It wasn't exactly equal but I said it was okay. Danny said the inside of the Dodge smelled like Doreen Lablanski, so he got a bottle of his brother's English Leather and sprinkled it all over the seats. We spent the afternoon riding around with the windows down.

For supper I ate three helpings of Lasagna and some tossed salad. Then I took a shower, buffed my Weejuns, creased my white ducks and put on my new Madras shirt. I picked up Danny and his date and drove to Nancy's house. Nancy's mother said Nancy had to be home by twelve and looked suspicious and Nancy said, "Okay Mom," but when she got in the car she called her mother a "pure-T bitch."

The movie was about Frankie and Annette at the beach and Annette was trying to make Frankie jealous by dating this English rock star who was really Frankie in disguise and somehow this motorcycle gang got all mixed up in it and I began to lose interest. I kissed Nancy but she had bad breath. I didn't want to make her angry, so I walked to the refreshment stand and bought some Doublemint which she chewed for about two minutes and spit out. It didn't help, so I just nibbled at her ear and fumbled with the three clasps on her bra but she wouldn't let me do anything because Danny was in the back seat. I got angry and started the car and took everybody home. Danny was pissed and said I owed him for the gas and I said, "Tough shit." At the front door Nancy wouldn't even hug me. "You know," she said, before going inside, "sometimes you can be a real jerk."

## For a Fifty-Three Dodge

That flathead six
got eight miles to the gallon
and the ball joints were so bad
my teeth rattled for thirty minutes
after we slapped the railroad tracks.
The stabilizer bar was bent
and the window cranks weren't connected
to anything and the seats were so sprung
I had to put two Coke crates
under the driver's side just to see
over the steering wheel.
Three times a brake line ruptured
and sent me screaming into busy intersections.

Still there was that rainy night
I kissed Nancy Simmons goodbye for good
and drove that Dodge into the dark.
The lights over South River blurred
like the eyes of an old lover turning away,
and I looked out through that cracked
windshield and believed, if only for a moment,
that the highway to anywhere
was wide open.

## Short Note on a Cat Sleeping

*for Nancy*

a sleeping cat hears every sound
you once told me

today the november wind rattles
the window glass
& I watch a cat sleeping
grey paws upturned
a leg buried beneath his thorax
like a knot of silk
his tufted ears waiting

I toss an empty beer can into
the waste basket
& not a whisker twitches

how nice
after all this time
to think of you & how you lied
to me about everything
including cats

## Senior Talent Night

Three fat girls
billed as Bell and
the Romantics
intoned a medley
from *Bye Bye Birdie*—
acappella.
Monk McGuinus,
front teeth blacked out,
played the ham bone
and smiled.
Mandy Williams strummed
a Silvertone solid body
and sobbed as she sang
"You'll Never Walk
Alone."
Then the eight of us,
all guys dressed
in outsized diapers,
lip synced "Twist and
Shout" and hit each other
in the face with
shaving cream pies.

Danny Chapman,
who was smarter (it was
his idea) and better
looking than I
hollered WHO-KA!
and hit me in the face
with a pie
so hard I got angry
and right there on

the stage I knocked
him down and beat
the hell out of him.
And they loved it,
loved it,
the applause meter
got goosed clear
off the scale.

It was a warm night
and the auditorium was gamy
with 800 crazed
teenagers.
We were what they wanted.
We were what they needed.
So we won ten dollars each
and got to do it again,
only this time
I took it easy
with the dukes.

Afterwards,
Miss Judy,
my fourth grade teacher,
came backstage,
shook my hand, smiled,
said, "Stephen, I always
knew that you'd amount
to something."

# Working for Dorsey

All that grayblue summer
the pungency of fresh paint
lingered like guilt.
"Cut in those moldings faster
and don't leave no holidays,"
Dorsey mumbled between clinched teeth,
his rum crook bobbing ash.

Rainy Saturdays we poured
Mary Carter Roll-Hide into
empty Sherwin-Williams cans
so Dorsey could jack up materials,
and as the sun lulled
over the Chesapeake
at a $1.10 an hour
I slapped on one coat of
egg-shell white and heard
Dorsey swear it was two:
"Lady, that job'll last ya
ten years, maybe more."

Those nights I dreamed of cheap
paint blistering in the August sun,
of needling autumn rain seeping
between buckled siding,
the damp bay wind chilling
the bones of children.

The summer I was seventeen
I painted houses for Dorsey,
then flew away from the peeling
sashes and twelve-hour days.
I remember how the aluminum
wing vibrated against a sky
gone gray as ash, and how,
as the plane described an
oblique ear-fiddling arc,
I looked down and saw those
pool-specked subdivisions
spread like lace
upon the Maryland countryside.

# I Visit Nancy Simmons at a Catholic Girls' College Saturday, April 26, 1969

Nancy took me to her room
and we were sipping wine on the balcony
when this dyslexic nun,
wild behind the wheel of a Camaro,
screamed into the parking lot
and eviscerated the dumpster,
spilling a week's worth of garbage
into the April wind.

The clap of cold metal
brought them out,
hundreds of chaste beauties
fondling rosaries and
smiling virginal smiles
I'd just imagined
behind those cloistered walls.

My God,
their best secrets danced
across the parking lot —
a snow storm of pornography,
naked bodies in a swirl
of foldouts and fornicating instant photos,
a cornucopia of smut novels,
blue movies, erotic prints, lace panties,
condoms, dildos,
maybe a fetus or two.

"Let's go inside," Nancy said,
so we closed the door
and she put her arms around my neck.
"Honey," she whispered,
"didn't anyone ever tell you
that what we covet in prayer
we take out in flesh?"

## The Great Depression

Because love
was never enough for you
I bought a six pack
of Schlitz and watched
this genuinely depressing movie
about the Great Depression.

It was winter.
Newspapers tumbled
down empty streets
and a small gray man,
his hands pushed deep
into his empty pockets
and his woolen cap
pulled over his eyes,
scuffed the pavement.

And it came to me
after the third beer
that in the movie of your
life I was that man.
You've never forgiven me
all my small debts—
the Andy Jacksons
I slapped into the palms
of surly doormen,
the mugs of bootlegged
beer I swilled,
the nights I jazzed away
in smoky speakeasies.

Well, listen up Nancy:
you can make all the movies
you want, but when you walk
those backlot streets
keep one beautiful blue eye open
for the long black Hudson.
That's me, the guy in the back seat
choking on the big cigar.

# How the World's Been Treating Them: January, 1970

*BT Barnhart:*

Do you remember Charlie Truette,
the red-haired boy
who worked at the Texaco station
and how when we went for ice cream
he'd lock his fingers between my fingers,
his palms against my palms
and then bend me slowly backward,
my wrists screaming,
my knees cracking,
buckling me down
onto the hot asphalt?

Do you remember how he smiled
as he did that?

*Danny Chapman:*

It began
the night I dropped my date,
a frigid redhead who'd talked
of nothing but old lovers,
and drove east on John Hanson
Highway while Jim Ritter
made it in the back seat of my
Corvair with a blonde who
whimpered.

It ended
five years later
on Baltimore Street
the night I got tattooed and laid.
The hooker lifted my wallet,
a doctor in Dundalk cured the clap,
the tattoo I've still got
just to remind me
it wasn't all for nothing.

## No Photograph

There is no photograph of my father,
the gunner's mate second class
suicided by Zekes one November
dawn in Lingayen Gulf,
and me, the conscientious objector
and believer in peace and love,
as we stood facing each other,
fists raised,
a week after Kent State,
in the back yard of the house
where I grew up,
the house where —
as my father kept reminding me —
I'd been fed, clothed and sheltered,
and where, on that May night,
he told me that I deserved to die,
deserved to bleed to death
face down on the macadam,
had I wandered, however innocently,
into the line of fire
when the National Guard —
those desperate gas-masked figurines
crouching, M-1's leveled,
in *Life*'s gauzy photograph —
ended all illusion,
made no difference, he said,
that I'd never waved a flag
or shot some disgruntled Guardsmen
the finger — all this as I frothed
with adolescent idealism and screeched
in a voice five octaves too high to endure
inane platitudes and fashionable cliches,

while my mother sobbed
and my wife cowered in the shadows,
our young son asleep in her arms,
oblivious as the dead
in Lingayen Gulf. Or Ohio.

# Wine and Cliches

What can I expect on a rainy afternoon
when I've drunk too much wine
except to think of how there are lives
that go wrong from the very beginning?
Take, for example, Linwood Thompson.
He and I were born in the same small town,
same hospital, same day,
our mothers wheeled into the delivery room
and the two of us arriving within seconds
of each other on a July morning
when there was not a breath of air
and not a soul about, except my father
who claims he was pacing a floor five
hundred miles away and Linwood's father
who was sitting on the curb of Washington
Street watching a frayed cloud line drift away.
I know this because at Linwood's funeral
his father described for me how the sun
misted the elms and poplars
just as we screamed ourselves alive.

It might have been otherwise, but Linwood
Thompson was nobody's favorite playmate.
He was simply too loud, too awkward
and too anxious to have a friend.
If you've read this far, I don't have
to tell the entire story: you knew a Linwood,
the class dipshit who was cracked with towels
as he danced, buttocks jiggling, from the shower
in the steamy locker room after gym,
after he'd been the last chosen for softball
and the first to drop an easy pop fly.

But that night at the funeral home
as his father waxed poetic, almost
as if to will the return of that July morning,
his hand resting lightly on the flag-covered
coffin, it all seemed pointless to me.
Not that my life, or any life, isn't trite,
but you can't be more commonplace than dead.
So it's raining this afternoon, I have nowhere
to go, and the wine bottle is half empty—
or half full, depending on how you like
your wine and cliches.

# Coming Back To the Old Emptiness

So my grandfather rises
from the depths of the Depression
to flail my father (then a child
younger than my small son)
with an electric cord
in the basement of the house
on College Avenue,
the scars visible fifty years later
on my father's back and thighs,
and etched deeper in all of us —
my brother, sister and mother —
than that night's rage
meant to inflict.

My grandfather is dying tonight,
the madness of eighty years —
the drunken women he dragged home,
the gamblers and bootleggers for whom
his family gave up their beds,
the endless, unrememberable
moments of cruelty
told now with a sigh and the
closing of my father's eyes —
all of it crumbling,
like the demolition of an old hotel
collapsing room by room,
coming down absolutely
but in a motion all too slow.

I could see it otherwise,
from a distance and with dispassion,
but for the night my grandfather,

a born-again Christian and ex-drunkard,
opened a drawer filled with knives,
guns, clubs, ice picks, razors —
a collection of murder weapons
purchased from a local magistrate —
and told me the story of each,
laughing at the moment of death,
then held a silver dagger lightly
to my throat, grains of sweat
beading in his palm.

Because we suffer impossible love,
my father grieves tonight for his father
just as I grieve for mine,
and my son, safe in his bed,
will learn of these cruelties
only in a poem, which itself must
someday crumble, its dust rising
in final dissolution.

## Most of What We Take Is Given

Believing that the abandoned farm houses
and burned-out mobile homes held no meaning,
I spent my twenty-second year driving between
the Piedmont and the Carolina coast,
my foot to the floorboard between the tiny
crossroads whose names were Hayne, Stedman,
and Gumbranch, my eyes on the highway,
counting the yellow lines that ticked by like
seconds till I'd see the woman I believed was
waiting.  These trips began in summer, heat devils
and tobacco blossoms shimmering, my mind
too manic to discern any singular detail,
but in the fall, a mile or so west of Beulaville
on a curve that dropped steeply down an escarpment,
I noticed a pony tethered to a fence post.
The pony was red, the color of the damp clay bank
against which it had, in all likelihood,
stood the previous summer, and I reasoned
that only the yellow poplar leaves drifting
the embankment served to silhouette the pony.
All that fall and early winter the pony
simplified my predicament: its suffering —
if indeed it was suffering — was not of its making,
and certainly it could will no circumstance.
It seemed unaware of the passing trucks
and cars, the weeks, the months, even the rain
that fell and turned its thick coat a dark brown.
And I began to believe that it all came down
to the casual drifting of leaves, a randomness
that must, finally, strip away all dignity.
Late winter brought ice storms, snow, mist
rising from the ditches and swamps, the Cape Fear
deep and filthy beneath the bridge I crossed

each Friday and Sunday. I recall an afternoon
in late February, the pony standing motionless,
wet snow clinging in heavy knots to its fur,
its eyes, as always, fixed on a patch of
gray earth. By then I knew it was ending.
I suspected, in fact, that the woman had taken
a new lover. I cannot now blame her, time and
distance being what they are, and it is best
to remember her standing in a doorway,
arms crossed below her breasts, her face
composed in silence, as if to ask a question.
It was April, and the highway west could
have been a green tunnel leading me anywhere.
I did not notice the red pony that afternoon,
and believe now that it had simply faded
into the sameness of the clay bank
against which it had stood waiting.